Superpowers for Entrepreneurs: Strategies for Getting Through the First Year and Taking Off

Copyright © 2024 Reginaldo Osnildo
All rights reserved.

PRESENTATION

THE FOUNDATION OF ENTREPRENEURIAL SUCCESS

KNOWING YOUR MARKET

EFFICIENT STRATEGIC PLANNING

FINANCIAL MANAGEMENT FOR ENTREPRENEURS

LOW COST, HIGH IMPACT MARKETING

THE ART OF SALE AND NEGOTIATION

BUILDING A STRONG BRAND

DIGITALIZATION AND ONLINE PRESENCE

CONTACT NETWORK AND STRATEGIC PARTNERSHIPS

THE POWER OF CUSTOMER FEEDBACK

INNOVATION AND CONSTANT ADAPTATION

TIME AND PRODUCTIVITY MANAGEMENT

HIRING AND TEAM MANAGEMENT

OVERCOMING CHALLENGES AND OBSTACLES

SUSTAINABILITY AND SOCIAL RESPONSIBILITY

MAINTAINING MENTAL HEALTH AND WELL-BEING

TECHNOLOGY AND TOOLS FOR ENTREPRENEURS

CONTINUOUS LEARNING AND PERSONAL DEVELOPMENT

BUSINESS EXPANSION AND SCALABILITY

PERFORMANCE EVALUATION AND SUCCESS METRICS

EFFECTIVE NETWORKING

PREPARATION FOR THE FUTURE AND INNOVATION

ENTREPRENEURIAL RESILIENCE

EMPOWERING YOURSELF FOR ENTREPRENEURIAL SUCCESS

REGINALDO OSNILDO

PRESENTATION

Welcome to the world of entrepreneurship, where every decision counts, every strategy makes a difference and the path to success is as challenging as it is rewarding. If you are taking the first steps on this journey, know that you are not alone. " **Superpowers for Entrepreneurs: Strategies for Getting Through the First Year and Taking Off** " is your definitive guide to navigating the turbulent seas of starting a business and emerging not just intact, but in a position of strength, ready to grow and expand.

This book is more than just a manual; is a compass to guide you through the complexities of modern entrepreneurship. Combining practical wisdom with innovative strategies, this resource is designed to prepare you for the unique challenges of freshman year and beyond. With each chapter, you'll discover the tools, knowledge, and inspiration you need to turn your vision into reality.

Through the pages of this book, you will learn how to build a solid foundation for your business, understand and take advantage of the market, create efficient strategic plans, and manage your finances accurately. Let's explore the power of low-cost marketing, the art of selling and negotiation, and the importance of building a strong brand. Together, we will dive into the digital world, expand your network of contacts, learn to value customer feedback, and much more.

Each chapter is a step forward in your entrepreneurial journey, designed to be complete in itself but also an integral part of a greater whole. At the end of each one, an invitation to the next step, ensuring a smooth transition and a continuous learning experience.

This book reflects my journey and the lessons learned along the way, updated for today's context and challenges. With a direct approach focused on you, the entrepreneur, "**Superpowers for Entrepreneurs: Strategies for Getting Through the First Year and Taking Off**" is your indispensable companion. Here, theory meets practice, inspiration merges with action, and the dream of running a successful business becomes a tangible goal.

Get ready to embark on this transformative journey. The chapters that follow are not just readings; They are stepping stones to your success. And the first step begins now, with the foundation of entrepreneurial success. Let's together uncover what it takes to build a business not just designed to survive, but to thrive in an ever-changing world.

Whether you're a dreamer, a doer, or both, "**Superpowers for Entrepreneurs: Strategies for Getting Through the First Year and Taking Off**" is your manifesto for success. The journey ahead is exciting, challenging and, most of all, possible. Let's start.

Yours sincerely

Reginaldo Osnildo

THE FOUNDATION OF ENTREPRENEURIAL SUCCESS

Every entrepreneur's journey begins with a dream, an idea that aspires to become something big. But, so that this dream does not fade away in the face of the first obstacles, it is essential to build a solid foundation. This chapter is dedicated to understanding the importance of establishing a firm foundation for your business, focusing on three fundamental pillars: mission, vision and values.

MISSION: YOUR WHY

Your mission is the heart of your business, the purpose that drives it. It's the reason you get up every morning and face everyday challenges. To define your mission, ask yourself:

- **Why does my company exist?**

- **What problem am I solving?**

- **How do I want to impact the world around me?**

Remember, the mission is more than words on paper; it guides your decisions and strategies, keeping you aligned with what really matters.

VISION: YOUR DESTINY

Vision is the long-term picture of what you want your business to become. She serves as a beacon, guiding her steps and keeping her team motivated, especially in difficult times. Your vision should be ambitious but achievable, inspiring growth and innovation.

To define your vision, visualize where you want your business to be in 5, 10 or 20 years. How will it impact your customers, your community, and perhaps even the world?

VALUES: YOUR MORAL COMPASS

Values are the principles that guide behavior and actions within your company. They create organizational culture and influence how your team interacts with each other and with customers. Your values should reflect what's most important to you and your business, whether that's integrity, innovation, excellence or compassion.

Identify three to five core values that will define the way your company operates. They will be crucial to building an authentic brand and generating trust among your stakeholders.

BUILDING YOUR FOUNDATION

With your mission, vision, and values defined, you have the foundation on which to build everything else. They will guide your strategies, help you make decisions and attract customers and employees who share your beliefs. Remember, a strong foundation is not just about surviving; it's about creating a lasting legacy.

With the foundation established, it's time to look outside and understand the world in which your business will operate. In the next chapter, we will dive into the art of knowing your market. Let's explore how to conduct effective market research, identify unmet demands, understand the competition, and discover opportunities to stand out. Preparing to understand your market is the next crucial step in turning your vision into reality. Together, we will discover how your mission, vision and values align with the needs and desires of your prospects, ensuring your business not only survives, but thrives in today's competitive environment.

Whether you're starting from scratch or looking to redefine your existing business, an in-depth understanding of the market is critical to your success. So, take a deep breath and prepare to dive into the rich opportunities that await you. Knowledge is power, and you're about to equip yourself with everything you need to make your venture a resounding success.

KNOWING YOUR MARKET

Now that you've established a solid foundation for your business, it's time to expand your vision to the outside world by delving into the ecosystem in which your company will operate. This chapter is dedicated to the importance of carrying out effective market research, a vital tool that will equip you with the knowledge needed to understand your customers, assess the competition and identify unique opportunities for growth.

THE IMPORTANCE OF MARKET RESEARCH

Market research is your beacon in the vast ocean of entrepreneurship. It helps reduce uncertainty, minimize risk and inform your strategic decisions. By deeply understanding who your customers are, what they value, and how they behave, you can develop products or services that directly meet their needs and wants.

UNDERSTANDING YOUR CUSTOMERS

The first step to effective market research is defining your target audience.

- Who are they?

- Where are they?

- What are your problems, needs and desires?

Tools like online surveys, interviews, and focus groups can provide valuable insights.

Once you have a clear understanding of your target audience, you can segment them into smaller groups with similar characteristics or needs. This allows for a more personalized approach to your marketing and product development strategies.

ANALYZING THE COMPETITION

Knowing who your competitors are and what they offer is crucial. A detailed competitive analysis can reveal gaps in the market that you can exploit. Look for weaknesses in your products or services and consider how you can differentiate your offering to fill those gaps.

Additionally, understanding your competitors' strategies can inspire new approaches for your own business. However, remember to focus on creating unique value for your customers, rather than simply copying what others are doing.

IDENTIFYING MARKET OPPORTUNITIES

With a solid understanding of your customers and competitors, you will be well positioned to identify market opportunities. Look for emerging trends that align with your mission, vision and values. This could include new technologies, changes in regulations or shifts in consumption patterns.

PUTTING RESEARCH INTO PRACTICE

Equipped with comprehensive market research, you are ready to make informed decisions about product development, pricing, distribution and marketing strategies. Remember that market research is not a one-time exercise; it should be an ongoing part of your strategic planning process to adapt to changing market conditions.

Knowing your market is just the beginning. In the next chapter, we will delve deeper into efficient strategic planning. You'll learn how to turn insights from market research into a robust action plan that will guide your company through its early years and beyond. Let's explore how to set clear objectives, map out your strategies and create a business plan that not only supports your growth ambitions but also prepares you for the challenges and opportunities ahead.

Whether you're refining your current offering or preparing to launch a new product or service, solid strategic planning is crucial to success. Join us in the next chapter, where we turn research into plan, vision into reality, ensuring your business is not only ready to take off, but also equipped to soar.

EFFICIENT STRATEGIC PLANNING

After diving deep into your market knowledge, it's crucial to turn these insights into actions. This chapter is dedicated to guiding you through the process of creating a robust business plan, which will not only serve as a roadmap for your company's early years but also as a tool for attracting investors, partners, and talent. Efficient strategic planning is what differentiates companies that thrive from those that merely survive.

THE IMPORTANCE OF A SOLID BUSINESS PLAN

A well-designed business plan is essential for any entrepreneur. It details your vision, mission, market strategy, financial analysis and operational plans, acting as a compass that guides all your business decisions. Furthermore, it is a vital communication tool for convincing external stakeholders of the value of your venture.

DEFINING YOUR GOALS

Before diving into the details of your plan, it's crucial to establish clear, achievable goals. These objectives must be specific, measurable, attainable, relevant and timely (SMART). By setting these parameters, you create a frame of reference that not only directs your strategies but also allows you to evaluate progress over time.

MAPPING YOUR STRATEGY

With your goals in hand, the next step is to develop strategies to achieve them. This includes identifying your target market, uniquely positioning your product or service, and defining your sales, marketing, and operations tactics. Each strategy must be designed to respond to the needs and desires of your target audience, differentiating you from the competition.

FINANCIAL PROJECTIONS

A critical component of your business plan is financial projections. They provide insight into the potential return on investment, including expected revenues, costs and break-even analysis. These projections help you set realistic financial goals and identify financing needs.

OPERATIONAL PLANS

Operational plans detail how your company will function on a day-to-day basis. This includes logistics, supply chain, production and distribution processes. Having a clear operational plan is crucial to ensuring efficiency and the ability to scale your operations as your business grows.

EVALUATION AND ADJUSTMENT

The business world is always changing, and your business plan must be flexible enough to adapt. Set regular milestones to review and adjust your plan as needed. This not only helps keep your business aligned with initial goals but also allows you to proactively respond to opportunities and challenges.

With a solid business plan in hand, you're ready to tackle the financial aspect of entrepreneurship. In the next chapter, we will cover financial management for entrepreneurs. You will learn strategies for managing your business finances effectively, including budgeting, cash flow and initial investments. These skills are vital to ensuring the financial health and long-term sustainability of your business.

Strategic planning does not end with the creation of a document; It is a continuous process of learning, adapting and growing. As we move into the next chapter, stay focused, determined, and open to new possibilities. The journey to entrepreneurial success is as much about the destination as it is about the journey. Let's continue sailing together.

FINANCIAL MANAGEMENT FOR ENTREPRENEURS

We now enter vital territory for the survival and prosperity of any business: financial management. In this chapter, we'll explore the essential strategies for keeping your company's finances healthy, from setting a budget to effectively managing cash flow and making initial investment decisions. Understanding and applying sound financial management practices not only protects your business against adversity but also paves the way for sustainable growth.

UNDERSTANDING FINANCIAL MANAGEMENT

Financial management involves planning, organizing, directing and controlling the company's financial activities. It is the foundation that supports all other areas of the business, from operations to marketing and sales. Effective financial management ensures that you have resources available for current needs while planning for the future.

SETTING UP A BUDGET

A well-planned budget is the first tool in your financial management arsenal. It provides a forecast of your income and expenses, allowing you to make plans based on realistic estimates. A budget helps you avoid overspending and ensure that resources are available to the areas that need them most. Start by listing all of your sources of income, followed by a detailed estimate of fixed and variable expenses. This will give you a clear picture of your financial situation and help you identify areas for cost reduction or increased revenue.

CASH FLOW IS KING

Effective cash flow management is crucial. It involves monitoring the inflow and outflow of cash to ensure you have enough working capital to cover daily operations. Positive cash flow means your business is in a healthy position to meet its financial obligations. Use a cash flow spreadsheet to predict and monitor financial movements, allowing proactive adjustments to maintain the financial health of the business.

INITIAL INVESTMENTS AND FINANCING

Determining how much money is needed to start and keep your business operating is a critical task. This includes capital for start-up costs such as equipment, inventory and marketing expenses, as well as a reserve to cover operations until the business becomes profitable. Explore diverse funding sources, including loans, angel investors, crowdfunding, or venture capital. Remember to carefully evaluate the terms and conditions of any financing to ensure they align with your long-term goals.

KEEPING CONTROL

Implement systems to monitor and control your finances. This may include accounting software, credit policies, regular audits and financial reviews. Having control over your finances allows you to identify trends, optimize resources and make informed decisions.

With the foundations of financial management established, you are ready to dive into the world of marketing. In the next chapter, we'll explore low-cost, high-impact marketing tactics. You will learn how to maximize the visibility and reach of your business on a limited budget, using creative and effective strategies. This knowledge will be crucial to attracting customers, building your brand and accelerating growth.

Financial management is the pulse of your enterprise, providing the means to operate, innovate and expand. As we move into the next stage of your entrepreneurial journey, keep sound financial practices at the heart of your business. After all, a financially healthy business is one that has the freedom and ability to reach its full potential. Let's move forward together, with our eyes on the bright future you are building.

LOW COST, HIGH IMPACT MARKETING

After establishing a solid foundation for the financial management of your venture, the next crucial step is to draw attention to your business. In this chapter, we'll explore effective marketing strategies that won't drain your financial resources but have the potential to make a significant impact on the market. Low-cost marketing is especially vital for startups and small businesses that operate on limited budgets but aspire to reach a wide audience and create a lasting connection with their customers.

UNDERSTAND YOUR TARGET AUDIENCE

Before starting any marketing campaign, it is essential to have a deep understanding of your target audience.

- **What are your needs, desires and behaviors?**

- **Where do they spend their time online and offline?**

A clear understanding of your audience will allow you to target your marketing strategies more effectively, increasing your return on investment (ROI).

CONTENT MARKETING

One of the most effective forms of low-cost marketing is content marketing. This involves creating and sharing valuable and relevant content to attract and engage your target audience. Blogs, videos, infographics, and podcasts are just a few of the ways you can provide value to your prospects, establishing your brand as an authority in your niche. Content marketing not only helps build trust and relationships, but also improves your online visibility through search engine optimization (SEO).

SOCIAL MEDIA

Social media is a powerful tool for low-cost marketing. Platforms like Facebook, Instagram, Twitter and LinkedIn offer the opportunity to connect with your audience in a direct and personal way. The key to success on social media is consistency and authenticity. Share stories that resonate with your followers, engage with them through comments and messages, and use paid ads strategically to expand your reach.

PARTNERSHIPS AND COLLABORATIONS

Forming partnerships with other companies or influencers who share a similar audience can be an efficient way to increase your visibility. Service exchanges, collaborative content or joint social media campaigns are ways to benefit both parties involved. These partnerships can help reach new audiences without the significant cost typically associated with customer acquisition.

E-MAIL MARKETING

Email marketing remains one of the most efficient and lowest-cost marketing tools available. By building an email list of potential and existing customers, you have a direct channel to communicate updates, special offers, and valuable content. The key to successful email marketing is personalization and relevance; make sure your messages meet your audience's specific needs and interests.

EVALUATE AND ADJUST

As with all business strategies, the key to successful marketing is to monitor, evaluate and adjust your campaigns based on performance. Use analytics tools to track engagement, conversions, and ROI, and don't be afraid to try new approaches to see what works best for your brand.

Equipped with low-cost, high-impact marketing strategies, you're ready to delve deeper into the art of selling and negotiation in the next chapter. The ability to sell is not only essential for business growth, but also for establishing lasting relationships with your customers. Let's explore practical techniques that will strengthen your selling and negotiation skills, ensuring you not only meet, but exceed your customers' expectations.

Effective marketing is about telling a story that resonates, building genuine connections and offering unparalleled value. With the right strategies, you can maximize the impact of your marketing campaigns, regardless of the size of your budget. Let's move forward with confidence, ready to sell our vision to the world.

THE ART OF SALE AND NEGOTIATION

Mastering the art of sales and negotiation is crucial to the success of any entrepreneur. This chapter is dedicated to honing these essential skills by offering you practical strategies to increase your effectiveness in sales and negotiations. Regardless of the sector or size of your business, the ability to sell your vision and negotiate efficiently can be the difference that puts your company ahead of the competition.

UNDERSTAND YOUR VALUE

The first step to selling effectively is understanding and communicating the unique value your product or service offers. Before approaching a customer or entering into a negotiation, be clear about what problems you solve, how you improve your customers' lives and what differentiates your offer from others available on the market. This understanding of value is the foundation of all your sales and negotiation interactions.

BUILD RELATIONSHIPS, NOT JUST TRANSACTIONS

Successful sales and negotiations are founded on strong relationships and trust. Focus on understanding your customers' needs and desires, offering solutions that align with their interests. A consultative approach, where you act more like an advisor than a traditional salesperson, can help establish a deeper connection and foster customer loyalty.

EFFECTIVE COMMUNICATION

The ability to communicate clearly and persuasively is vital. This includes listening carefully, asking relevant questions, and expressing your ideas concisely. In negotiations, understanding and using nonverbal communication techniques, such as eye contact and body language, can also reinforce your message and help build rapport.

NEGOTIATION STRATEGIES

When negotiating, it is important to enter with a win-

win mentality, seeking solutions that benefit both parties. Be prepared, know your limits, and be willing to make reasonable concessions without compromising the core value of what you are offering. Tactics like anchoring, where you set a high starting point of reference, can be helpful, but should always be used with the goal of reaching a fair agreement.

OVERCOME OBJECTIONS

Objections are a natural part of the selling and negotiation process. Instead of seeing them as obstacles, see them as opportunities to deepen your understanding of the customer's needs and adjust your proposal accordingly. Be prepared to respond to common objections with accurate information and clear benefits of your product or service.

CLOSURE

Effectively completing a sale or negotiation requires clarity, confidence and sometimes creativity. Learn about different closing techniques and be prepared to use the most appropriate one based on the situation and client. Remember, closing is just the beginning of a business relationship that you want to nurture and grow.

Now that you are equipped with fundamental selling and negotiation strategies, the next chapter will guide you through the process of building a strong brand. A well-built brand not only facilitates the sales process, but also creates a memorable identity that can elevate your business above the competition. Let's explore how to develop and promote your brand in a way that resonates with your target audience and sustains the long-term growth of your business.

Selling and negotiation are arts that, when practiced with skill and integrity, can lead to the establishment of fruitful and lasting business relationships. By applying the strategies in this chapter, you will be well positioned to turn prospects into valuable partners and customers into loyal advocates for your brand. Let us move forward now with confidence, ready for the next step in our entrepreneurial journey.

BUILDING A STRONG BRAND

Building a strong brand is essential to stand out in a competitive market. A well-developed brand not only facilitates the sales and negotiation process, as described earlier, but also creates a memorable identity that can elevate your business. In this chapter, we'll explore effective strategies for developing and promoting your brand, ensuring it resonates with your target audience and sustains the long-term growth of your business.

DEFINING YOUR BRAND IDENTITY

Your brand identity is the sum total of how your brand looks, feels, and communicates to the world. This includes your name, logo, color scheme and any other visual elements, as well as the tone of voice used in your communication. These elements must be consistent across all customer touchpoints, from your website to your packaging and marketing materials, to create a cohesive brand experience.

COMMUNICATE YOUR VALUES

Your brand should reflect the values and mission of your business. Today's customers are looking for more than just products or services; they want to connect with brands that share their values and aspirations. Effectively communicating these values in your brand message can help establish an emotional connection with your audience, increasing brand loyalty and advocacy.

DIFFERENTIATE YOURSELF FROM THE COMPETITION

A strong brand stands out from the competition. Ask yourself: What makes my business unique? Whether it's a unique value proposition, an innovative product, or an exceptional commitment to customer service, make sure your brand clearly communicates what sets it apart. Use brand stories to highlight these differentiators in an engaging and memorable way.

BUILD ONLINE PRESENCE

A strong online presence is crucial for brand building. This includes a professional website that reflects your brand identity, as well as active social media profiles where your target audience spends time. Content shared online should be valuable and relevant to your audience, helping to establish your brand as an authority in your niche. SEO strategies are also key to ensuring your brand is easily found online.

ENGAGE WITH YOUR AUDIENCE

Audience engagement helps build strong relationships and foster brand loyalty. This can be done through content marketing, social media interactions, loyalty programs, and excellent customer service. Listening to your audience and responding to their comments, questions and concerns demonstrates that you value their opinion and are committed to their satisfaction.

MONITOR AND ADAPT YOUR BRAND STRATEGY

Brand building is not a static process. It's important to monitor how your brand is perceived in the market and adapt your strategy as necessary. Customer feedback and analytics tools can provide valuable insights into your brand's performance and areas for improvement.

With a strong brand as your ally, the next step is to expand your presence in the digital world. In the next chapter, we will explore digitalization and online presence, where you will learn how to establish an effective online presence, including website, e-commerce and social media strategies. A solid digital presence is essential for reaching potential customers, building lasting relationships and driving your business growth.

Building a strong brand is an ongoing journey that requires consistency, creativity and commitment. By following the strategies outlined in this chapter, you'll be well-positioned to develop a brand that not only tells your business' story but also meaningfully connects with your audience. Let's move forward, ready to take our brand into the digital world and beyond.

DIGITALIZATION AND ONLINE PRESENCE

In today's digital age, having a strong online presence is not only advantageous; it's essential. This chapter is dedicated to guiding you through the steps to establish and optimize your online presence, ensuring that your brand is not only found, but also stands out in the vast digital space. From creating an impactful website to effectively managing social media, we will cover the fundamental strategies for capturing the attention of your target audience and driving meaningful engagement.

DEVELOPING AN ATTRACTIVE WEBSITE

Your website is often the first point of contact between your brand and potential customers, acting as a 24/7 digital representative of your business. Therefore, it must be visually appealing, easy to navigate, and optimized for conversions. This means including clear calls to action (CTAs), easily accessible contact information, and a responsive design that ensures a consistent user experience across devices.

SEO: OPTIMIZING FOR VISIBILITY

Search engine optimization (SEO) is crucial to increasing your website's visibility in organic searches. This involves using relevant keywords, improving page loading speed, and ensuring that your site is easily indexable by search engines. Effective SEO not only increases traffic to your website, it also helps you attract more qualified visitors who are more likely to convert into customers.

EFFECTIVE E-COMMERCE STRATEGIES

For businesses that sell online, a robust e-commerce strategy is vital. This includes offering a safe, intuitive and hassle-free online shopping experience. Elements like detailed product descriptions, high-quality images, streamlined checkout processes, and accessible customer service options can significantly improve the shopping experience and increase conversion rates.

MAXIMIZING THE POTENTIAL OF SOCIAL MEDIA

Social media is a powerful tool for building and promoting your brand online. Choose platforms that your target audience uses most and create content that encourages interaction, such as posts, videos and stories. The key is to be consistent and authentic, establishing a recognizable brand voice and social presence that encourages follower engagement and loyalty.

ANALYSIS AND ADAPTATION

Use analytical tools to monitor the performance of your online presence and adapt your strategies based on real data. This could include adjusting your SEO approach, refining your social media content, or optimizing the user journey on your website. Continuous analysis is essential to understand what works, what doesn't, and where there are opportunities for improvement.

With a solid online presence established, the next step is to strengthen and expand your network of contacts. In the next chapter, we will discuss the importance of building a solid network of contacts and how to form strategic partnerships that can boost your business growth. Effective networking not only opens doors to new opportunities, but also provides valuable support and insights as you navigate the path to entrepreneurship.

Establishing an effective online presence is an ongoing journey that requires dedication, creativity and flexibility. By implementing the strategies covered in this chapter, you will be well positioned to capture your target audience's attention, build lasting relationships, and position your brand for long-term success in the digital environment. Let us move forward, ready to connect, collaborate and grow on our entrepreneurial journey.

CONTACT NETWORK AND STRATEGIC PARTNERSHIPS

With a robust online presence now established, it's time to turn our attention to the power of human connections. This chapter is dedicated to the art of building an effective network and developing strategic partnerships that can drive the growth of your business. Navigating the entrepreneurial ecosystem requires more than just a solid idea and a digital presence; it's also about who you know, how you connect and collaborate to achieve common goals.

THE IMPORTANCE OF A STRONG CONTACT NETWORK

A strong network gives you access to new opportunities, resources, knowledge and support. It can open doors to strategic partnerships, new markets, talent and investments. Start by attending industry events, conferences and webinars, both virtually and in person. Social media also offers a powerful way to connect with industry peers, thought leaders and potential customers.

EFFECTIVE NETWORKING

Effective networking is based on creating mutually beneficial relationships, not just collecting contacts. Show genuine interest in the people you meet by actively listening and sharing knowledge and experiences. Remember that networking is a two-way street; Think about how you can help others, just as they can help you.

DEVELOPING STRATEGIC PARTNERSHIPS

Strategic partnerships can range from formal agreements with other companies to less formal collaborations with industry influencers or organizations. The objective is to find partners whose objectives, target audience and values are aligned with those of your business. These partnerships can lead to joint projects, shared marketing campaigns, or even new product developments.

TIPS FOR SUCCESSFUL PARTNERSHIPS

- **Identify potential partners:** Look for companies or individuals that complement your product/service offering and that could benefit from collaboration.

- **Set clear goals:** Make sure both parties have clear, shared goals for the partnership.

- **Communicate effectively:** Maintain open and clear lines of communication, ensuring all expectations are understood and agreed upon.

- **Monitor and evaluate:** Establish metrics to evaluate the success of the partnership, adjusting the strategy as necessary.

Armed with a solid network and strategic partnerships in place, the next step is to focus on the importance of customer feedback. In the next chapter, we'll explore how to collect, analyze, and act on customer feedback to continually improve your products, services, and overall customer experiences. Feedback is an invaluable tool for growth and innovation, allowing you to refine your offering and further strengthen your brand.

Building and maintaining an effective network of contacts and developing strategic partnerships are ongoing processes that can significantly accelerate the growth of your business. By applying the strategies covered in this chapter, you are positioning yourself to not only expand your reach, but also create a supportive ecosystem that can take your business to new heights. Let us move forward, ready to value and act on feedback from our customers, the true voice behind our success.

THE POWER OF CUSTOMER FEEDBACK

As we move along the entrepreneurial journey, one of the most valuable assets you can collect is customer feedback. This chapter focuses on how to effectively collect, analyze, and implement customer feedback to continually improve your products, services, and the overall customer experience. Listening and acting on customer feedback not only demonstrates that you value their opinions, it is also essential to the innovation and sustainable growth of your business.

COLLECTING CUSTOMER FEEDBACK

There are several effective ways to collect customer feedback, including online surveys, feedback forums on your website, focus groups, and social media monitoring. It's important to offer multiple platforms for feedback, ensuring you capture the voice of a wide range of customers. Additionally, encourage feedback by making the process as easy and accessible as possible and considering rewards for those who take the time to provide their opinions.

ANALYZING THE FEEDBACK RECEIVED

Once collected, the next step is to analyze the feedback systematically to identify patterns, recurring problems and opportunities for improvement. Data analysis tools and feedback management software can help categorize and prioritize feedback, making it easier to identify areas that require immediate attention.

ACTING BASED ON FEEDBACK

Implementing customer feedback is where many companies face challenges. Prioritize changes based on their feasibility, potential impact, and alignment with long-term business objectives. Additionally, it is crucial to communicate back to customers what was done in response to their feedback. This not only closes the feedback loop, but also builds trust and loyalty by showing that you take their opinions seriously.

CREATING A CULTURE OF CONTINUOUS FEEDBACK

Integrating customer feedback into decision-making and product development is essential to creating a culture of continuous improvement. Encourage your team to view feedback as an opportunity to learn and grow, not criticism. Regularly revisit and reevaluate how you collect and use feedback to ensure the process remains effective and aligned with your business needs.

With a solid system for collecting and implementing customer feedback in place, the next step is to focus on constant innovation and adaptation. In the next chapter, we will cover strategies to keep your business innovative and adaptable to market changes. In a business world that is always evolving, the ability to innovate and adapt is not just a competitive advantage, but a necessity for long-term survival and growth.

By prioritizing customer feedback, you are not only optimizing your offering to better meet current market needs, but you are also building a solid foundation for future success. Let's move forward, ready to embrace innovation and adaptability as the main drivers of our continued growth.

INNOVATION AND CONSTANT ADAPTATION

In a rapidly evolving business world, the ability to innovate and adapt to market changes is more than a competitive advantage; it is a necessity for long-term survival and growth. This chapter explores strategies to keep your business at the forefront of innovation, ensuring you remain relevant, resilient and able to seize new opportunities as they arise.

CULTIVATING AN INNOVATION MENTALITY

Innovation starts with the right mindset. Encourage a culture that values curiosity, experimentation and continuous learning within your team. Foster an environment where calculated risk-taking is supported and where failures are viewed as opportunities for growth and learning. The innovation mindset allows your team to think outside the box and explore new ideas without fear.

REMAINING AGILE AND ADAPTABLE

Adaptability is key in an ever-changing business environment. This means being able to respond quickly to market trends, customer needs and new technologies. Develop flexible processes and be open to pivoting your strategy when necessary. Business agility allows you to capitalize on emerging opportunities and minimize risks in a timely manner.

FOSTERING INNOVATION THROUGH COLLABORATION

Innovation often comes from collaboration, whether within your team, with clients or through strategic partnerships. Create spaces to exchange ideas and collaborate with partners outside your industry to gain new perspectives. Strategic partnerships, especially, can offer shared resources, knowledge and networks that drive innovation and open new avenues for growth.

INTEGRATING TECHNOLOGY

Technology plays a crucial role in innovation and adaptation. Stay tuned for the latest technological trends that could benefit your business, whether through process automation, improving the customer experience or exploring new market channels. Integrating emerging technologies can not only streamline your operations but also create innovative products or services that distinguish your brand.

MEASURING SUCCESS AND ITERATING

Establish clear metrics to evaluate the success of your innovation initiatives. Use data and customer feedback to iterate and refine your strategies. The innovation process is continuous; What works today may not work tomorrow, so it is vital to maintain an iterative approach, always looking to improve and adapt.

With a solid approach to innovation and adaptation established, the focus turns to time management and productivity. In the next chapter, we will explore techniques for maximizing productivity and managing time efficiently. Not only does this help ensure you and your team can stay innovative and adaptable, but it also supports overall wellbeing and job satisfaction.

Constant innovation and adaptation are fundamental to entrepreneurial success in the 21st century. By implementing the strategies discussed in this chapter, you will position your business to not only survive market changes, but to thrive in them. Let us move forward, ready to embrace the techniques that will boost our efficiency and productivity to new heights.

TIME AND PRODUCTIVITY MANAGEMENT

Effective time management and increased productivity are essential to maintaining innovation and adaptability, enabling you and your team to maximize your efforts and achieve your business objectives. This chapter offers strategies for optimizing your time management and improving productivity, ensuring that critical tasks receive the attention they deserve and that team well-being is maintained.

EFFICIENT PRIORITIZATION

The first step to effective time management is learning to prioritize tasks based on their urgency and importance. Use the Eisenhower Matrix method to categorize tasks into four quadrants: Important and Urgent, Important but Not Urgent, Not Important but Urgent, and Not Important and Not Urgent. This helps you focus on the activities that truly drive your business goals, while avoiding procrastination on less critical tasks.

PRODUCTIVITY TECHNIQUES

There are several techniques for increasing productivity, including the Pomodoro method, which involves working intensely for short periods followed by brief breaks. Another technique is the two-minute rule, which encourages immediate completion of tasks that can be completed in two minutes or less, quickly eliminating minor distractions.

TIME MANAGEMENT TOOLS

Technology offers a variety of tools and applications designed to help with time management and productivity. Project management tools like Trello , Asana , and Monday.com can help organize tasks, set deadlines, and track the team's progress. Additionally, apps like RescueTime can monitor how you spend your time on the computer, offering insights to improve your work habits.

EFFECTIVE DELEGATION

Delegation is a crucial skill for leaders and entrepreneurs. Identify tasks that can be delegated to team members, freeing up your time to focus on high-value activities. When delegating, be clear about expectations and offer the resources necessary to complete the task. This not only increases efficiency, but also contributes to the professional development of your team.

MAINTAINING BALANCE

As you strive to improve your time management and productivity, it's crucial to maintain a healthy work-life balance. Set clear boundaries between work time and personal time, and encourage your team to do the same. Proper balance promotes well-being and prevents burnout, keeping everyone motivated and productive in the long term.

Now that we've covered the importance of time management and productivity, the next step is to focus on hiring and managing teams. In the next chapter, we'll explore strategies for recruiting, training, and managing a team that shares your venture's vision. A well-managed team is the backbone of any successful business, empowering your company to reach new heights of success.

Effective time management and productivity are more than just techniques and tools; they are a mindset that empowers you and your team to achieve more while maintaining a high level of satisfaction and well-being. By implementing the strategies discussed in this chapter, you are one step closer to creating a work environment that not only values efficiency, but also balance and job satisfaction. We move forward now, ready to build and manage a team that will be the driving force behind our continued success.

HIRING AND TEAM MANAGEMENT

The strength of any business lies in its team. Building, training and managing a team that shares your venture's vision not only strengthens the foundation of your business, but also drives innovation and growth. This chapter covers essential strategies for recruiting the right talent, developing their skills, and keeping them engaged and motivated.

RECRUITMENT: FINDING THE RIGHT TALENT

The recruitment process begins with clearly defining the profile of the ideal candidate, considering not only the necessary technical skills, but also the personal characteristics and values that align with your company's culture. Utilize multiple recruitment channels, including online job platforms, professional social media and internal referral programs, to attract a wide range of candidates.

INTERVIEWS AND SELECTION

The interview process is crucial to assess not only the candidate's competence, but also their compatibility with the company culture. Use behavioral questions to understand how the candidate has handled past situations and situational questions to assess how he or she would handle future challenges. Including team members in interviews can also provide valuable perspectives and facilitate new employee onboarding.

ONBOARDING AND TRAINING

Once hired, an effective onboarding program is essential to integrate the new member into the team and company culture. Providing comprehensive training not only on specific job responsibilities, but also on company values, processes and expectations, helps ensure a smooth transition and increases long-term productivity.

TALENT DEVELOPMENT AND RETENTION

Continuous development of your team is essential to maintain engagement and motivation. Offer opportunities for professional growth, such as training courses, workshops and challenging projects. Recognize and reward achievements to promote job satisfaction and loyalty. Talent retention also depends on a positive work environment, where feedback is encouraged, and conflicts are managed constructively.

PERFORMANCE MANAGEMENT

Performance management is an ongoing process that involves setting clear expectations, regularly monitoring performance and providing constructive feedback. Set specific, measurable, achievable, relevant, and timely (SMART) goals and conduct regular performance reviews to discuss progress, challenges, and action plans for improvement.

With a well-built and effectively managed team, the next challenge is to face and overcome the obstacles that arise in the path of business growth. In the next chapter, we will cover strategies for overcoming challenges and obstacles, ensuring that your business remains resilient and adaptable in the face of adversity.

Building and managing a team requires dedication and a strategic approach to ensure everyone is aligned with the company's mission and values. By implementing the strategies discussed in this chapter, you will be prepared to build a team that not only shares your vision, but is also committed to the collective success of the business. Let us move forward now, ready to face together the challenges that await us, with the confidence that our team is our greatest strength.

OVERCOMING CHALLENGES AND OBSTACLES

Every enterprise faces challenges and obstacles on its way. Whether dealing with competition, facing financial difficulties or overcoming internal crises, the ability to face and overcome these difficulties is what defines a resilient and successful business. This chapter covers strategies for identifying, facing and overcoming challenges that may arise, ensuring that your business not only survives, but thrives in the face of adversity.

IDENTIFYING CHALLENGES EARLY

The first step to overcoming challenges is to identify them as early as possible. Keep an eye on changes in the market, consumer behavior and the internal performance of your business. Analytics tools and constant feedback from customers and staff can be valuable in spotting signs of potential problems before they become unmanageable.

ANALYSIS AND PLANNING

Once you identify a challenge, take time to understand its roots and potential impact on your business. This involves collecting data, consulting with your team and, if necessary, seeking external advice. Based on this analysis, develop an action plan that addresses the problem directly, considering different scenarios and preparing for possible repercussions.

FLEXIBILITY AND ADAPTATION

The ability to adapt quickly to changing circumstances is crucial to overcoming challenges. This could mean pivoting your strategy, exploring new markets or adjusting your business model. Encourage a culture of flexibility within your team, where innovation is valued and new ideas are welcomed.

LEARNING FROM CHALLENGES

Each challenge offers a learning opportunity. Analyze the situations your business has faced to identify valuable lessons about what worked, what didn't, and how you can improve in the future. This continuous learning process is essential for the growth and development of your business.

MAINTAINING RESILIENCE

Resilience is perhaps the most important quality for an entrepreneur to face challenges. This involves maintaining a positive attitude, even in the face of adversity, and persisting in your long-term goals. Strengthen your resilience by taking care of your well-being and that of your team, maintaining a strong support network and remembering your purpose and passion that drove the creation of your business.

With strategies to overcome challenges well established, the next step is to focus on incorporating sustainable and socially responsible practices into your business. In the next chapter, we'll explore how sustainability and social responsibility can not only benefit the environment and society, but also strengthen your brand and promote the long-term success of your business.

Overcoming challenges and obstacles is an inevitable part of entrepreneurship. By approaching these moments with preparation, resilience and the ability to learn and adapt, you strengthen your business against future adversity. Let us move forward now, ready to embrace practices that guarantee us not only success, but also a positive impact on the world around us.

SUSTAINABILITY AND SOCIAL RESPONSIBILITY

Integrating sustainable and socially responsible practices is increasingly recognized not only as an ethical imperative, but also as a smart business strategy. Companies that embrace these principles demonstrate a commitment to the well-being of the planet and society, while building a strong brand that resonates positively with consumers, investors and the broader community. This chapter discusses how to incorporate sustainability and social responsibility into your business in ways that benefit both the world and your bottom line.

UNDERSTANDING SUSTAINABILITY AND SOCIAL RESPONSIBILITY

Sustainability refers to the ability to meet the needs of the present without compromising the ability of future generations to meet their own needs. Corporate social responsibility (CSR) involves ethical and conscious conduct of business, considering its environmental, social and economic impact. Both concepts overlap in the quest to create a positive impact, in addition to achieving business objectives.

BENEFITS OF INCORPORATION OF SUSTAINABLE PRACTICES

- **Brand differentiation:** Sustainable and socially responsible companies stand out, attracting customers who value these principles.

- **Operational efficiency:** The implementation of sustainable practices often leads to cost reduction, through resource savings and process optimization.

- **Talent attraction and retention:** Many professionals prefer to work for companies that demonstrate concern about social and environmental impact.

- **Long-term resilience:** Businesses that consider their environmental and social impact tend to be more resilient and adaptable to global changes.

STRATEGIES TO IMPLEMENT SUSTAINABILITY AND CSR

- **Assess your impact:** Start with an audit of your company's current environmental and social impact. This may include energy consumption, resource use, impact on the local community, among others.

- **Set clear goals:** Based on your assessment, set clear goals for impact reduction, community improvement, and corporate governance.

- **Engage your team:** Sustainability and CSR must be incorporated into the company's culture. Train your team on the importance of these practices and how they can contribute.

- **Communicate your efforts:** Share your sustainability initiatives and progress with customers, partners and the community. This not only reinforces your commitment, but also encourages others to follow a similar path.

With an established commitment to sustainability and social responsibility, the next step is to ensure the mental health and well-being of those who make your business thrive. In the next chapter, we will address the importance of taking care of mental health and well-being in the workplace, offering strategies to create a healthy and productive work environment.

Incorporating sustainability and social responsibility into your business is not just about doing good; It's about doing business well. As we move forward, remember that the decisions we make today shape the world we live in tomorrow. Ready to take the next step, we now move forward to focus on the well-being of our team, recognizing that the true strength of a business lies in its people.

MAINTAINING MENTAL HEALTH AND WELL-BEING

Mental health and well-being are fundamental to the sustainable success of any business. Healthy, happy employees tend to be more productive, creative and engaged. This chapter focuses on the importance of promoting mental health and well-being in the workplace, offering practical strategies for creating a culture that values and supports the well-being of all team members.

UNDERSTANDING THE IMPORTANCE OF WELL-BEING

Well-being at work goes beyond avoiding stress; it's about creating an environment that promotes satisfaction, engagement and personal fulfillment. When employees feel supported with their mental health needs, they perform better, show greater company loyalty, and contribute to a positive work environment.

STRATEGIES TO PROMOTE MENTAL HEALTH AND WELL-BEING

- **Promote mental health awareness:** Educate your team about the importance of mental health, demystifying stigmas and promoting a culture of openness and support. Workshops, lectures and informational resources can be helpful.

- **Offer support and resources:** Make resources such as counseling or psychological support available, either internally or through partnerships with mental health service providers. Employee assistance programs (EAPs) can be a valuable addition to company benefits.

- **Create a positive work environment:** Foster an environment that values open communication, collaboration and recognition. Management practices that encourage positive feedback and celebration of achievements boost morale and well-being.

- **Encourage work-life balance:** Promote flexible work policies, such as flexible hours or the possibility of remote work, helping employees better manage their personal and professional responsibilities.

- **Promote healthy habits:** Encourage healthy practices in the workplace, such as regular breaks, physical activity and healthy eating. Breakout spaces, wellness activities and health initiatives can contribute significantly to the overall well-being of staff.

MONITORING AND ADAPTING

It's important to regularly monitor your team's well-being, using satisfaction surveys, mental health assessments and direct feedback. Be open to adjusting policies and practices based on what you learn, keeping well-being at the center of your company culture.

With an established commitment to mental health and wellbeing in the workplace, the next step is to explore how technology and modern tools can make running your business easier. In the next chapter, we'll discuss "technology and tools for entrepreneurs", covering innovative solutions that can increase efficiency, improve communication and drive growth for your business.

Maintaining mental health and well-being is essential to developing a resilient and motivated team, capable of facing challenges and achieving goals successfully. By implementing the strategies discussed in this chapter, you not only promote a healthy work environment, but you also strengthen your business's foundation for sustainable success. We move forward now, ready to embrace technology as an ally in our continued growth.

TECHNOLOGY AND TOOLS FOR ENTREPRENEURS

In today's digital age, technology plays a crucial role in almost every aspect of running a business. From optimizing operations to improving communications and boosting marketing, the right technology tools can deliver significant competitive advantages. This chapter explores innovative solutions that can help entrepreneurs increase efficiency, improve customer management, and facilitate sustainable business growth.

PROJECT MANAGEMENT TOOLS

Tools like Asana, Trello, and Monday.com allow teams to organize tasks, track progress, and collaborate efficiently, all on a unified platform. These solutions facilitate the delegation of tasks, establish clear deadlines and offer visibility into the progress of projects, ensuring that everyone is aligned and focused on the objectives.

CRM SOLUTIONS

Customer Relationship Management (CRM) systems like Salesforce, HubSpot, and Zoho CRM help manage and analyze customer interactions across the entire lifecycle. By centralizing customer data, these tools provide valuable insights into behaviors and preferences, allowing you to personalize communication and improve the customer experience.

COMMUNICATION AND COLLABORATION TOOLS

Platforms like Slack, Microsoft Teams and Zoom are essential for effective internal and external communication. They offer features ranging from instant messaging and video calling to file sharing, facilitating real-time collaboration regardless of the team's location.

MARKETING AUTOMATION

Marketing automation tools like Mailchimp, Marketo, and ActiveCampaign let you create, manage, and optimize marketing campaigns. These solutions can automate emails, segment audiences, track interactions, and provide detailed analytics on campaign performance, improving marketing ROI.

E-COMMERCE SOLUTIONS

For businesses that sell online, e-commerce platforms like Shopify, WooCommerce and Magento offer powerful features for creating and managing online stores. They make everything from creating product listings to processing payments and managing shipping easier, providing a smooth shopping experience for customers.

DATA ANALYSIS AND BI

Data analysis and Business Intelligence (BI) tools, such as Google Analytics, Tableau and Power BI, allow you to collect, process and visualize large volumes of data. These tools provide insights that can help make informed decisions, identifying market trends, evaluating campaign performance, and optimizing business strategies.

Equipped with the right technology tools, the next step is to focus on continuous development of skills and knowledge. In the next chapter, we will cover "continuous learning and personal development", highlighting the importance of continuous education and personal growth to maintain competitiveness and relevance in a constantly evolving market.

Adopting innovative technology and tools is essential to navigating today's business environment, enabling entrepreneurs to optimize operations, improve customer satisfaction and drive growth. As we move forward, remember that technology is an enabler, but the true driver of success remains the vision and dedication of the entrepreneur. Let us move forward now, ready to explore how continuous learning can prepare us for the challenges and opportunities ahead.

CONTINUOUS LEARNING AND PERSONAL DEVELOPMENT

In a rapidly changing business environment, the ability to learn and adapt is indispensable. Continuous learning and personal development are not only fundamental to maintaining competitiveness; they also fuel innovation, resilience, and growth both personally and professionally. This chapter highlights the importance of continuing education and offers strategies for incorporating personal development into an entrepreneur's routine.

CULTIVATING A GROWTH MENTALITY

Adopting a growth mindset means recognizing that your skills and intelligence can be developed with effort, time and dedication. See challenges as opportunities to learn, not as insurmountable barriers. This approach promotes resilience and motivation to pursue ambitious goals, in addition to encouraging the constant search for knowledge and improvement.

STRATEGIES FOR CONTINUOUS LEARNING

- **Set learning objectives:** Set clear learning goals that align with your career aspirations and your business goals. This may include developing specific skills, obtaining certifications, or delving deeper into relevant areas of knowledge.

- **Take advantage of online resources:** Access to educational resources has never been wider. Platforms like Coursera , edX , Udemy and LinkedIn Learning offer courses on a variety of topics, many of which are taught by world-renowned institutions.

- **Participate in networks and communities:** Engaging with communities and professional networks can provide learning through the exchange of experiences, mentoring and networking. Attending industry events, workshops, and seminars are also great ways to stay up to date on trends and best practices.

- **Reflective practice:** Take time to reflect on your experiences, successes and failures. Reflection is a crucial part of the learning process, allowing the internalization of lessons learned and the application of new knowledge in future situations.

- **Encourage team development:** Promote a culture of learning within your organization by encouraging team members to pursue their own personal and professional development. This may include allocating a budget for training, creating individualized development plans, or offering dedicated time for learning.

With an established commitment to continuous learning and personal development, the next step is to contemplate expanding your business. In the next chapter, we'll discuss "business expansion and scalability", exploring strategies for planning expansion sustainably and scaling up your operations to meet growing demand.

Continuous learning is the fuel for innovation and long-term success. By investing in your own development and that of your team, you not only enrich your skills and knowledge, but also ensure that your business remains dynamic, adaptable and prepared for the challenges of the future. Let us move forward now, ready to explore the growth and expansion opportunities that await our venture.

BUSINESS EXPANSION AND SCALABILITY

Expanding a business is a significant milestone in any entrepreneur's journey. It is the result of hard work, continuous innovation and a well-executed strategy. However, growing in a sustainable and scalable way requires careful planning, adequate resources and the ability to adapt to market changes. This chapter explores key strategies for planning your business expansion and effectively scaling your operations.

ASSESSING READINESS FOR EXPANSION

Before embarking on an expansion strategy, it is crucial to assess whether your business is truly ready to grow. This includes having a solid base of loyal customers, efficient operational processes and a team capable of handling increased demand. Furthermore, the financial health of your business must be robust enough to support the investment required for expansion.

DEFINING CLEAR EXPANSION OBJECTIVES

Identify what you want to achieve with the expansion. This can range from entering new geographic markets, diversifying the product or service line, to increasing production capacity. Setting clear, measurable objectives helps you focus your efforts and resources where they can have the greatest impact.

EXPLORING EXPANSION STRATEGIES

- **Geographic expansion:** Entering new markets can offer significant opportunities for growth. Conduct detailed market research to understand local needs and preferences and adjust your product or service offering as needed.

- **Product/service diversification:** Developing new products or services that complement your existing offering can open up new revenue streams and strengthen your market position.

- **Partnerships and strategic alliances:** Collaborating with other companies can facilitate entry into new markets, expand your customer base and improve operational efficiency.

- Franchising and licensing: For some businesses, offering franchises or licensing your brand and business model to third parties can be an effective way to expand with a relatively smaller investment.

ENSURING SCALABILITY

As your business grows, it is vital that your operations can scale efficiently. This may require automating processes, investing in technology or hiring more employees. Plan ahead to ensure the quality of your product or service is maintained, even as demand increases.

MONITORING PROGRESS AND ADAPTING

Closely track the progress of your expansion strategy through key performance metrics (KPIs) and be ready to adjust your plan as needed. The business environment is dynamic, and the ability to adapt quickly can be decisive for the success of expansion.

Having established a solid plan for expanding and scaling your business, the next step is to ensure you can effectively measure that success. In the next chapter, we will cover "performance assessment and success metrics", focusing on how to define, monitor and interpret the key indicators that will guide your business towards its long-term goals.

Expanding a business is an exciting journey, full of opportunities and challenges. With proper planning, a dedicated team and a focused strategy, you can significantly increase the chances of your expansion being successful. Let us move forward now, equipped to evaluate our progress and adjust our course as we navigate the ever-evolving future of entrepreneurship.

PERFORMANCE EVALUATION AND SUCCESS METRICS

As your business grows and evolves, a clear understanding of your performance becomes essential for continued success. This chapter focuses on the importance of establishing and monitoring success metrics, allowing you to evaluate the effectiveness of your strategies, make informed decisions, and adjust your course as necessary to achieve your long-term goals.

DEFINING RELEVANT SUCCESS METRICS

The first step to effective performance measurement is identifying which success metrics are most relevant to your business. These metrics can vary significantly depending on your company's industry, business model, and specific goals. Some common metrics include revenue, profitability, customer satisfaction, customer retention, and operational efficiency. Choose indicators that directly reflect progress towards your strategic objectives.

IMPLEMENTING MONITORING SYSTEMS

With the metrics defined, the next step is to implement systems to monitor these indicators consistently. This may involve the use of data analysis software, CRM tools (Customer Relationship Management) and other information technology systems that automatically collect and analyze data. Ensure data collection is accurate and reliable to adequately inform business decisions.

DATA ANALYSIS AND INTERPRETATION

Data collection is just the first part of the process; the analysis and interpretation of this data is what really allows you to understand how your business is performing. Learn to read trends in data, identify patterns, and extract actionable insights. This can reveal areas of success, as well as opportunities for improvement and necessary adjustments to your strategies.

CONSTANT FEEDBACK AND ADJUSTMENTS

Performance evaluation is not a one-time event, but an ongoing process. Use success metrics to provide regular feedback to your team, celebrate achievements, and discuss areas for improvement. Be prepared to make adjustments to your strategies and operations based on insights gained from your success metrics. The ability to adapt quickly based on real feedback is crucial in a dynamic business environment.

Now that you've established a solid system for evaluating the performance and monitoring the success of your business, the next step is to maximize your networking opportunities. In the next chapter, we'll explore "effective networking," providing strategies for building and nurturing professional relationships that can open new doors and accelerate your business's growth.

Assessing performance and understanding your success metrics are essential practices that inform the strategic direction of your business. They provide a solid foundation for making informed decisions, ensuring your business not only achieves, but exceeds its objectives. Let's move forward now, ready to expand our network of contacts and explore new opportunities that await us.

EFFECTIVE NETWORKING

Effective networking is an art and a science that can open new doors for your business, creating opportunities for partnerships, sales, mentoring and much more. This chapter offers guidance on how to build and cultivate a valuable professional network, emphasizing the quality of connections, reciprocity, and building genuine relationships.

UNDERSTANDING THE VALUE OF NETWORKING

Networking goes beyond simply exchanging business cards or adding on LinkedIn. It's about establishing meaningful connections that can bring long-term mutual benefits. A strong network can provide access to expertise, market insights, resources, support and growth opportunities.

STRATEGIES FOR EFFECTIVE NETWORKING

- **Be authentic:** Authenticity is fundamental. Show genuine interest in the people you meet by actively listening and engaging in meaningful conversations.

- **Offer value:** Networking is a two-way street. Think about how you can help others, whether by offering your expertise, sharing resources or connecting people.

- **Prepare an elevator speech:** Have a short speech prepared about yourself and your business, highlighting what makes you unique and how you can be a valuable resource to others.

- **Use social media to your advantage:** Platforms like LinkedIn are powerful tools for networking. Post relevant content, participate in discussions, and keep your profile updated and professional.

- **Attend networking events:** Conferences, workshops and industry events are great opportunities to meet people with similar interests and goals. Virtually or in person, these events can be valuable for expanding your network.

CONTACT MAINTENANCE

- **Follow Up :** After meeting someone new, follow up with a message or email, reiterating how much you appreciated the conversation and expressing interest in staying in touch.

- **Stay present:** Keep in regular contact with your network, sharing updates, asking about their projects, and offering help when appropriate.

- **Give thanks:** Always be grateful for any assistance, advice or resource you receive. A simple thank you can go a long way in strengthening a relationship.

With a strategic approach to networking and building a solid network in place, you are well positioned to face the future with confidence. In the next chapter, we'll focus on "future-proofing and innovation", exploring how you can anticipate trends and innovate within your business to stay ahead in an ever-changing market.

Effective networking is an essential skill in an entrepreneur's toolbox. By developing and nurturing professional relationships, you create a solid foundation for the success and longevity of your business. Let's move forward now, ready to embrace the future with a strong network and a mindset focused on innovation.

PREPARATION FOR THE FUTURE AND INNOVATION

In a rapidly changing business world, being prepared for the future and prioritizing innovation are crucial aspects of keeping your business relevant and competitive. This chapter explores how to anticipate market trends, adapt to change, and continually innovate to ensure your business not only survives, but thrives in the dynamics of the future.

ANTICIPATING MARKET TRENDS

Staying up to date with the latest industry trends is key to anticipating changes and identifying emerging opportunities. This can be achieved through:

- **Continuous research:** Make market research an ongoing activity. Use industry reports, trade publications, and analyst insights to stay informed.

- **Community Engagement:** Actively participate in industry forums, conferences and workshops. Listening and exchanging ideas with colleagues can offer valuable insights into where the market is moving.

- **Competitor monitoring:** Observe your competitors' innovations and strategies. This not only provides market insights but also inspiration to differentiate your offering.

ADAPTING TO CHANGES

Flexibility and adaptability are essential to navigate constant market changes. Some strategies include:

- **Culture of agility:** Promote a culture that values agility and the ability to respond quickly to changes. This involves everything from organizational structure to operational processes.

- **Continuous feedback:** Maintain open lines of communication with customers and staff for real-time feedback. This allows for quick adjustments to products, services or strategies.

- **Scenario planning:** Develop plans for various future scenarios, considering different market possibilities. This prepares your company to respond effectively to any situation.

CONTINUOUSLY INNOVATING

Innovation should not be seen as a single project, but as an integrated component of your business strategy. To foster continuous innovation:

- **Encourage ideas:** Create an environment where everyone in the company feels comfortable proposing new ideas. This could involve regular brainstorming sessions, suggestion boxes or internal innovation programs.

- **Test and learn:** Implement a test and learn approach to explore new ideas. Rapid prototypes and product/service pilots allow you to test concepts in the real market with minimal risk.

- **External collaboration:** Consider partnerships with startups, universities or research institutes. These collaborations can bring new perspectives and access to innovative technologies.

With a proactive strategy to predict the future and constantly innovate in practice, the next step is to strengthen the resilience of your business. In the next chapter, "entrepreneurial resilience", we will focus on developing the ability to bounce back from setbacks, stay motivated and persist in the face of challenges, ensuring the long-term sustainability of your venture.

Future-proofing and innovation are essential to successfully navigate the waves of change that characterize the modern business environment. By taking a proactive approach and cultivating a culture of innovation, you put your business in a strong position to capitalize on future opportunities and face challenges with confidence. Let us move forward now, ready to build a foundation of resilience that will sustain our continued success.

ENTREPRENEURIAL RESILIENCE

Resilience is the ability to recover quickly from difficulties; for entrepreneurs, it is an indispensable quality. This chapter covers how to develop entrepreneurial resilience, enabling you and your business to overcome setbacks, adapt to unexpected changes, and stay motivated in the face of challenges.

UNDERSTANDING ENTREPRENEURIAL RESILIENCE

Entrepreneurial resilience is not just about weathering storms, but also about growing from them. It involves the ability to maintain a positive outlook, learn from failures, and use challenging experiences as stepping stones to new opportunities.

STRATEGIES FOR BUILDING RESILIENCE

- **Cultivate a positive mindset:** See challenges as opportunities for learning and growth. A positive attitude helps you navigate difficult times and see beyond immediate setbacks.

- **Establish a support network:** Maintain close relationships with mentors, fellow entrepreneurs and a trusted team. A strong support network provides valuable advice, encouragement, and outside perspectives at critical times.

- **Embrace flexibility:** Be open to change and willing to adjust your strategies as needed. Flexibility allows you to quickly adapt to new information or circumstances.

- **Develop problem-solving skills:** Hone your ability to identify problems, generate creative solutions, and make informed decisions under pressure.

- **Stay focused on your long-term goals:** Even in the face of setbacks, keep your long- term goals clear. This provides a sense of direction and helps maintain motivation.

PERSONAL CARE AS THE FOUNDATION OF RESILIENCE

- **Prioritize your physical and mental health:** Self-care

is crucial for resilience. This includes eating healthy, exercising regularly, getting adequate rest, and practicing mindfulness or meditation.

- **Establish limits:** Learn to say no and establish healthy boundaries between work and personal life. This helps prevent burnout and ensures you have time to recharge.

- **Seek help when necessary:** Recognizing when you need help and seeking professional support is a sign of strength. Whether for business challenges or personal issues, seeking guidance can provide new solutions and relief in times of stress.

As we close this chapter, we are prepared to revisit the lessons learned and apply them to our own entrepreneurial journey. In the final chapter, "Empowering Yourself for Entrepreneurial Success," we'll reflect on the key insights from this book and how you can apply these principles to turn your entrepreneurial vision into reality.

Each success story is a testament to the power of the entrepreneurial spirit, the importance of never giving up in the face of challenges and the ability to transform failures into foundations for the future. Let us move forward now, inspired and equipped with the knowledge to forge our own path to success.

EMPOWERING YOURSELF FOR ENTREPRENEURIAL SUCCESS

Throughout this book, we explore many facets of the entrepreneurial journey, from building a solid foundation to overcoming challenges and exploring new frontiers for growth and innovation. This final chapter is an invitation to reflect on the lessons learned and consider how you can apply these insights to turn your entrepreneurial vision into a successful, tangible reality.

REFLECTION ON THE JOURNEY

Each chapter in this book offered strategies, advice, and inspiring stories designed to guide, inspire, and prepare you for the challenges and opportunities of entrepreneurship. Revisiting these lessons periodically can help you stay focused, adapt to new circumstances, and continue to grow both personally and professionally.

APPLYING LESSONS LEARNED

- **Build on a solid foundation:** Remember the importance of establishing a clear mission, vision and values that guide all your business decisions.

- **Know your market:** Stay informed about industry trends and your customers' needs to offer relevant and innovative solutions.

- **Be prepared to adapt and innovate:** The business world is constantly changing. Cultivate flexibility and a growth mindset to explore new opportunities.

- **Invest in relationships:** Build a solid network of contacts and keep an engaged team. People are the key to the success of your business.

- **Prioritize well-being:** Both your own well-being and that of your team are essential to maintaining long-term productivity and motivation.

MAINTAINING MOTIVATION AND FOCUS

The path to entrepreneurial success is full of ups and downs. Maintaining motivation and focus in the face of adversity is crucial. Celebrate the small victories, learn from the failures, and always keep your end vision in mind.

LOOKING TO THE FUTURE

The end of this book marks just the beginning of your entrepreneurial journey. Face the future with confidence, armed with the knowledge, skills and determination to overcome challenges and achieve your goals. Remember that success is not a destination, but a journey of constant learning, adaptation and growth.

" **Superpowers for Entrepreneurs: Strategies to Get Through the First Year and Take Off** " is designed as a guide to navigating the entrepreneurial journey with wisdom, effectiveness, and courage. The strategies and lessons shared here are designed to empower you to turn your ideas into actions, your actions into results, and your results into a lasting legacy. Move forward with passion, perseverance, and an unwavering commitment to your dreams. The world waits for the unique mark that only you can leave.

CONTINUING YOUR JOURNEY

Here are some steps you can take to continue your journey:

- **Reflect on your learning:** Take time to reflect on the concepts, strategies, and stories shared in this book. Which lessons resonated most with you? How can you apply them to your business?

- **Action plan:** Based on your reflection, develop a detailed action plan to apply these learnings. Set clear goals, specific steps, and deadlines to implement the strategies that seem most promising for your business.

- **Seek community:** Entrepreneurship can be a lonely journey, but it doesn't have to be. Look for communities of entrepreneurs, whether online or locally. These networks can offer support, resources, and opportunities for collaboration.

- **Commitment to continuous growth:** Learning never ends. Commit to continued growth, both personal and professional. Continue seeking knowledge, challenging yourself and adapting to market changes.

- **Share your story:** As you progress, share your own journey. Your experiences can inspire and guide other entrepreneurs just starting out. Consider blogging, speaking at events, or even mentoring other entrepreneurs.

Each entrepreneur follows a unique path, full of their own victories, challenges and learnings. True success comes not just from the results achieved, but from the growth experienced along the journey and the positive impact your business has on others and the world.

May this book be a beacon on your entrepreneurial journey, illuminating the path ahead with hope, inspiration, and practical guidance. Remember: the future is bright for those who dare to dream big, work hard, and remain resilient in the face of adversity.

Move forward with confidence, creativity and courage. The next chapter is yours to write, and the world is waiting to see what you create.

Good luck!

As we turn the final page of this journey together, I sincerely hope that the learnings shared here have touched your heart and sparked new perspectives. If this book has brought you any value, I kindly ask that you take a few moments to leave a review on Amazon. Your words not only help me grow and hone my craft, but they also guide other readers in their quests for knowledge and inspiration. Your opinion is a valuable gift, both for me and for the community of readers looking for stories that transform. I sincerely thank you for sharing this journey with me and I hope we can meet again in the pages of a new adventure.

REGINALDO OSNILDO

Hello, I'm Reginaldo Osnildo, author and innovator in the fields of sales, technology, and communication strategies. My background spans from the academic setting, as a professor and researcher at the University of Southern Santa Catarina, to hands-on strategy development at the Catarinense Radio Group. With a PhD in sales narratives and digital convergence, and a Master's in storytelling and social imaginary, I offer my readers a unique blend of theory and practice. My aim is to deliver knowledge in a simple, practical, and didactic language, encouraging direct application in one's personal and professional life.

Yours sincerely

Reginaldo Osnildo

+55 48 991913865

reginaldoosnildo@gmail.com

www.ingramcontent.com/pod-product-compliance
Lightning Source LLC
Chambersburg PA
CBHW070351230526
45471CB00006B/2522